Life Cycles

Written by Sally Morgan

Contents

Collins

D0813146

What is a life cycle?

An animal's life cycle starts when it's born. The young animal grows and gets larger until it becomes an adult. Then the animal reproduces to create more animals. This marks the beginning of the next life cycle.

Some animals, especially insects, have very short life cycles that are completed within a few weeks. But larger animals, such as mammals, have much longer life cycles that take many years to complete. For example, a female elephant may not be ready to reproduce until she's 20 or more years old. Some animals, such as the salmon, only reproduce once and then die. Others may reproduce many times during their lives.

Mosquitoes have one of the shortest life cycles – about three days.

3

Many animals start life as an egg, for example goldfish, blackbirds and crocodiles. The eggs hatch into young animals that grow to become adults. Other animals, such as lions, give birth to live young.

Insects, such as butterflies, have a more complicated life cycle. The butterfly life cycle starts with an egg that hatches into a larva called a caterpillar. This is the growing stage of the life cycle. However, caterpillars look nothing like adult butterflies. This means their bodies have to go through a stage where they're completely rearranged to become adults. This amazing change is called **metamorphosis**.

caterpillar

butterfly

5

Salmon

Salmon are large, powerful fish that are designed for speed. The shape of their body is a bit like a torpedo – it's long and gets narrower towards the tail. This streamlined shape slips effortlessly through the water.

Like all fish, a salmon has fins which help it to swim and stay upright in the water. There are two sets of paired fins, called the pectoral and pelvic fins, which help the fish to steer. There is a dorsal fin on the back, which stops the fish from rolling over in the water. One of the most important fins is the tail fin. This helps the fish to push through the water.

Did you know?
One of the largest salmon ever found was a chinook. It weighed 38 kilograms.

tail fin

adipose fin

dorsal fin

lateral line

gill flap

anal fin

pelvic fin

pectoral fin

mouth

All fish have gills for breathing in water. They use them to pick up oxygen in the water. The gills look a bit like feathers, and they're red because they contain lots of blood. The gills are found behind the head and they're protected by a flap. Water enters the mouth and flows through the gills, where the oxygen is picked up by the blood. Then the water passes out under the flap.

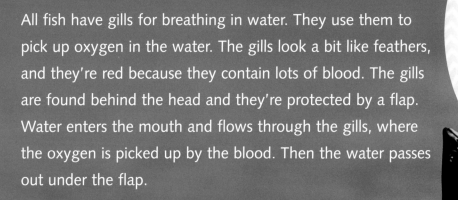

water

gill

Salmon are unusual fish as they're born in fresh water, but spend their adult lives in salt water. There are two main groups of salmon. Atlantic salmon, found in the Atlantic Ocean, and Pacific salmon, found in the Pacific Ocean. There are different species, or types, of Pacific salmon, including the cherry, chinook, chum, coho, pink and sockeye salmon.

Laying eggs

Salmon lay their eggs in fresh water, that is, water we can drink and which does not have much salt in it, unlike salty sea water. The female salmon look for streams and shallow rivers where water flows quickly over gravel. These places are called **spawning grounds**. Fast-flowing water carries more oxygen than slow-flowing water, which is important as the eggs need a steady supply of oxygen, otherwise they die.

The salmon arrive at the spawning grounds in the autumn and the females search for the perfect place to build their nests. Then, the female lies on her side on the gravel and uses her powerful tail to dig her nest, which is called a redd. With each beat of her tail, she removes a handful of small stones. Then she lays hundreds of small, round eggs in the nest. The eggs are immediately **fertilised** by a male who is waiting close by. Then the female moves upstream a little and does this again. As she digs out another nest, the gravel is tossed over the eggs lying in the first nest. The gravel hides the eggs from **predators**. Each female builds several nests and lays thousands of eggs.

A large female salmon lays as many as 7,000 eggs.

Hidden in the gravel

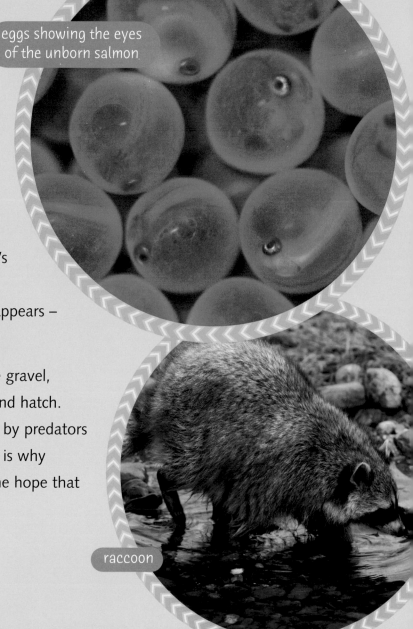

eggs showing the eyes of the unborn salmon

The eggs lie hidden in the gravel for about three months. They have to survive the icy water and at times they may be buried under a thick layer of snow and ice. The eggs are pale pinky-orange with a partly see-through soft shell. They're just a few millimetres in **diameter**. Inside, there's a large egg yolk that's rich in **nutrients**. After about four weeks, a large black dot appears – the eye of the unborn salmon.

Although the eggs are hidden amongst the gravel, only about ten in every 100 eggs survive and hatch. Some die from disease, but most are eaten by predators such as other fish, birds and raccoons. This is why the female salmon lays so many eggs, in the hope that a few will make it through the winter.

raccoon

When the tiny fish inside the egg are ready to hatch they move around and push out through the soft shell. They're barely two centimetres long and have a large yolk sac attached to the underside of their body. These tiny fish are called alevins and they remain hidden amongst the gravel. For the next week or two, they feed on the yolk which contains all the nutrients they need to grow. Eventually the yolk sac disappears.

Now the alevins are ready to move away, but they have a problem. They cannot float in the water yet. So, they beat their tails and push themselves to the surface to gulp some air. The air is used to fill their swim bladder, a balloon-like structure in their body that allows them to swim up and down in the water. These small salmon are now called fry.

alevins

Shark eggs

Not all fish lay small eggs. Many sharks lay a small number of very large eggs. Each egg is protected by a tough rubbery case. The egg of the **dogfish** is called a mermaid's purse. There are four **tendrils** that wrap around seaweed so that the egg does not get carried away.

baby dogfish swimming out of its mermaid's purse

adult dogfish

12

Other egg layers

Fish are not the only animals that lay eggs. Other egg layers include insects, **amphibians**, reptiles and birds. Amphibians, such as frogs, lay eggs that are protected by a thick coat of jelly. The jelly stops the eggs from drying out and makes it difficult for predators to eat them. The common frog lays a mass of eggs called frogspawn. It takes less than two weeks for the eggs to develop into tadpoles, which wiggle their way out of the jelly.

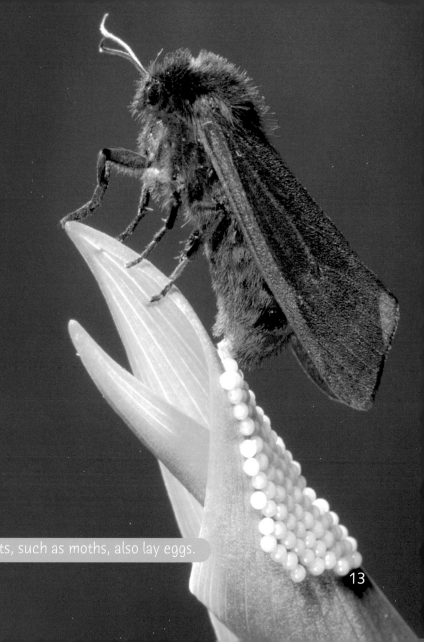

Insects, such as moths, also lay eggs.

13

Birds lay eggs that have a hard shell. The female bird sits on her eggs to keep them warm. When it's time to hatch, the tiny chick breaks through the shell with a special egg tooth on its beak.

chicks hatching from their eggs

The egg of the crocodile is about the same size as
a hen's egg, but it has a leathery rather than a hard shell.
Female crocodiles bury their eggs in a nest in
the ground and guard them until they hatch.
After their young have hatched,
the females help them out of the nest
and carry them to water.

Did you know?
The largest egg
belongs to the ostrich.
Each egg weighs
about 1.4 kilograms.
It's equivalent to about
24 chicken eggs.

15

Fish fry

The next stage in the life cycle of the salmon is the growing stage, when they are known as fry. The salmon fry are strong enough to leave the safety of the gravel. Over the next few months they drift slowly downstream, stopping to feed in places where the water is still.

Without the yolk sac, the fry look like miniature fish with a long body and tiny fins. They have to be careful as they're small and are hunted by many predators. They hide under rocks and amongst the vegetation in the water. During this time they feed mostly on plankton. Plankton is made up of tiny plants and animals that float in the water. It's an important food for many river animals.

The salmon fry's main enemies are predatory fish such as pike. But there are hunting insects too, such as water beetles that have vicious jaws. Herons and other wading birds stand in the water watching for the tiny fry as they dart around. This is a dangerous time for the salmon fry and only a few will survive until their first birthday.

heron standing in water

water beetle

17

Fingerlings

Once they reach one year of age, the young salmon are called parr, or fingerlings, because they're about the size of a finger. They have vertical markings along the side of their body, which look a bit like fingerprints. These dark markings provide camouflage which helps them to blend into the shadows so that they're not noticed by predators. The fingerlings live further down the river, feeding on larger prey such as insects that drop into the water from overhanging branches.

The time spent as fingerlings in the river varies depending on the species. The chinook and pink salmon only spend a few months as a fingerling, while the sockeye salmon spends the longest, up to four years.

19

Water memories

An important part of this growing stage is something called imprinting.
The fry memorise all the features of their home river – the type of rock,
the presence of boulders and the plant life. The water has a unique scent
which they remember when they return in the future to breed.

20

Unfortunately, people make changes to rivers. For example, the vegetation along river banks may be cleared to make way for bridges and river-front homes. The water may be polluted by harmful chemicals from agriculture and industry. This changes the scent of the water so that the salmon become confused when they return.

Other growing stages

There are growing stages in all life cycles. The kitten is the growing stage of the cat, while the puppy is the growing stage of the dog. The kitten and puppy look like little cats and little dogs. They grow from the time they're born until they reach full size and stop growing. Then they're ready to breed and produce young of their own.

The life cycle of the frog involves three stages – egg, tadpole and adult. The adult frogs lay their eggs in water and they hatch into tadpoles. The young tadpole starts off life looking a bit like a fish with a long tail, rather than a frog. Its body has to change into one of a frog. First, hind legs appear and then a pair of front legs. The tail gets shorter and disappears and, finally, the tiny froglet is ready to leave the pond.

adult frog

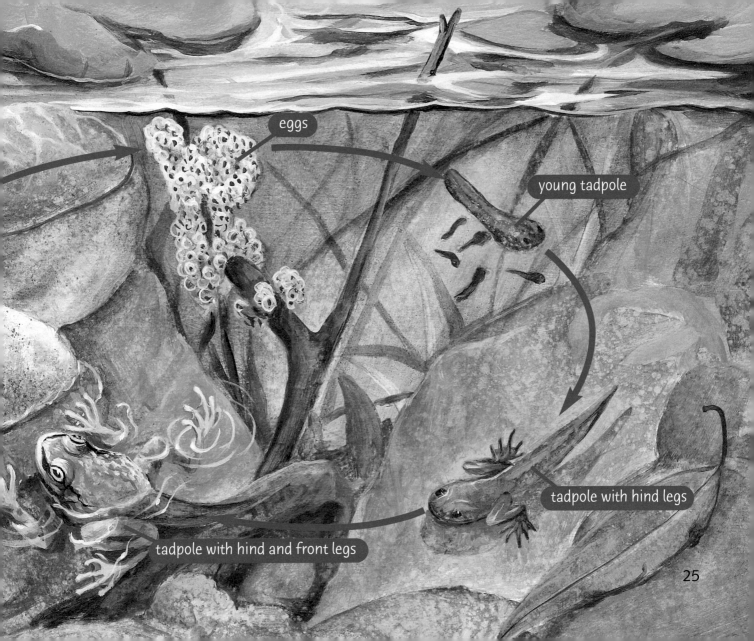

eggs

young tadpole

tadpole with hind legs

tadpole with hind and front legs

25

The life cycle of the butterfly is even more complicated, with four stages. It starts life as an egg that hatches into a caterpillar. The caterpillar feeds all the time, so it grows quickly. Finally, the caterpillar becomes a **pupa**. The pupa does not move and has a tough protective covering. It looks as if nothing is happening, but inside, the body of the caterpillar is changing into one of an adult butterfly. The body shape changes and the wings grow. Then the pupal case splits and an adult butterfly emerges.

butterfly

egg

caterpillar

pupa

27

Smolting

The salmon fingerlings gradually make their way downstream to the estuary, where the fresh water of the river meets the salt water of the ocean. They time their arrival carefully, so that they get to the estuary in spring. This is a time when the waters of the estuary are full of plankton, so there's plenty of food for them. Now they become smolts and prepare for the biggest change in their lives.

It's easy to tell if salmon fingerlings have become smolts from their appearance. The black markings down their side disappear and they become silvery all over. This is because they're preparing to live at sea. The brown markings are great for hiding in vegetation and on the river bed, but not so good in the deep water of the ocean. The silvery colour is better as it makes the salmon difficult to spot in the water. The shape of their body changes too, becoming longer and the fins darker. The young salmon are now about 15 centimetres long.

There are changes happening inside the smolts' bodies too, as they have to prepare for life in salt water. This is called smolting. Until now, the salmon have lived in fresh water. Fish living in fresh water have a problem of too much water entering their bodies. The freshwater salmon have to get rid of all the excess water through their **kidneys**. This means they produce lots of liquid waste in the form of urine.

In salt water the opposite is true. The salmon are surrounded by salty water and all the food and water they take in is salty too. The salmon have to try to keep the water in their bodies, so their kidneys work slowly and they produce very little urine.

The smolts live in the estuary for up to a year, getting used to the salt water and feeding on the rich supply of plankton, before heading out to the open ocean.

Life at sea

The smolts swim out to sea, where they grow into adults. They live together in small groups called shoals. Often they swim hundreds of kilometres to feeding grounds where there are lots of small fish and shrimp-like animals called krill.

The Pacific salmon swim across the Pacific Ocean to spend their adult lives feeding in the Gulf of Alaska and the Bering Sea. The Atlantic salmon leave rivers in Western Europe and the eastern side of North America and swim to feeding grounds near Greenland.

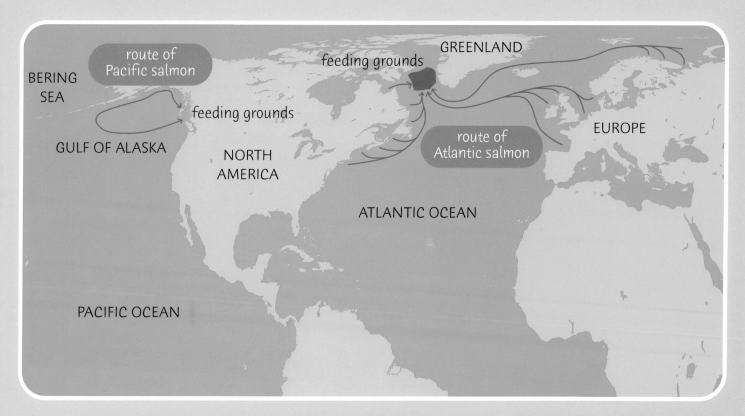

GREENLAND

feeding grounds

route of
Pacific salmon

BERING
SEA

feeding grounds

EUROPE

GULF OF ALASKA

NORTH
AMERICA

route of
Atlantic salmon

ATLANTIC OCEAN

PACIFIC OCEAN

Adult salmon spend several years at sea, feeding and growing, before they're ready to return to fresh water to spawn. When chinook and Atlantic salmon are fully grown they weigh up to 30 kilograms or more, but the sockeye salmon is much smaller and only weighs between two and a half and seven kilograms.

Life at sea is not safe. There are many predators in the water that hunt salmon. The younger salmon have to avoid larger predatory fish, while the adults are preyed upon by seals, sharks, dolphins and killer whales as well.

35

Ocean food chains

Salmon are an important part of the ocean food chain. A food chain is the feeding relationship between plants and animals. In the diagram below, the arrows show who eats who, except for the plant plankton, which make their own food from sunlight, just like plants on land.

killer whale

salmon

sunlight

plant plankton

animal plankton

small fish

37

These tiny plant plankton, which float in the ocean, are at the bottom of all ocean food chains. They are eaten by animal plankton, tiny marine animals that include crab and shrimp larvae, baby fish and jellyfish.

Plankton like to live in cool water where there are lots of **currents** that bring nutrients up from the seabed. There's so much plankton in some parts of the ocean that the water becomes a cloudy green colour. The oceans with the most plankton are found towards the North Pole and the South Pole. For this reason, many animals, including the salmon, swim to these waters to feed. Animal plankton is eaten by larger animals such as krill and small fish. These animals in turn are eaten by larger fish, like the salmon.

North Pole

plankton

South Pole

Did you know?

Sockeye salmon meat is orange-red because they eat so many krill of this colour while at sea.

38

At the top of the food chains are the largest hunters of the oceans –
the top predators. There are always fewer top predators than there are
prey animals. These top predators are expert hunters. They swim quickly
through the water because prey such as salmon are fast swimmers too.
They have well-developed senses so that they can find their prey in
the huge open ocean.

salmon shark eating a salmon

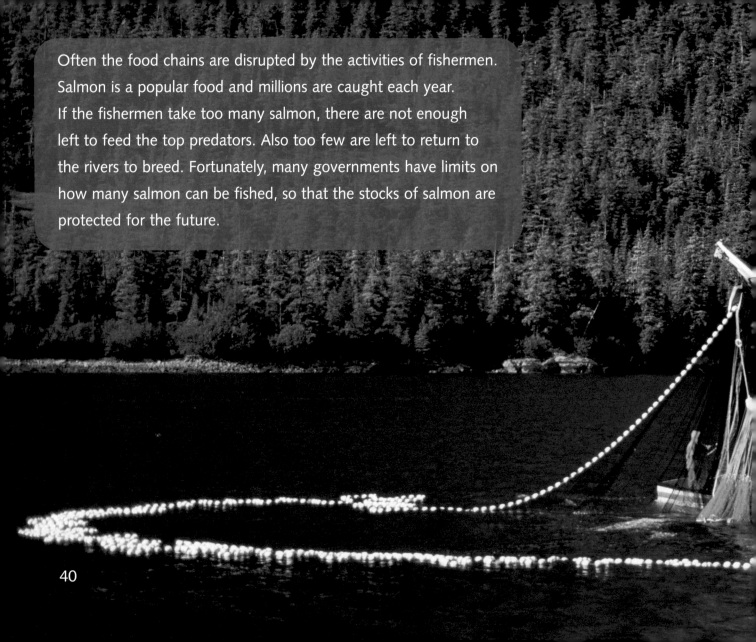

Often the food chains are disrupted by the activities of fishermen. Salmon is a popular food and millions are caught each year. If the fishermen take too many salmon, there are not enough left to feed the top predators. Also too few are left to return to the rivers to breed. Fortunately, many governments have limits on how many salmon can be fished, so that the stocks of salmon are protected for the future.

Returning home

Salmon stay in the oceans for up to eight years, feeding and growing. Each year, they swim thousands of kilometres in search of food and this keeps them very fit. They build up their fat stores too. This prepares them for the long journey when they return to the rivers of their birth to spawn and die. They swim back across the ocean looking for the smell of the water of their home river. From the time the salmon enter their home river until the time they spawn, they do not eat. Instead, they survive on the fat stored in their bodies.

Once salmon have been in fresh water for a while, they change appearance again. The sockeye salmon undergoes a very marked change.

42

sockeye salmon at sea

They change in colour from a silvery blue-grey to red, with a green head.
These bright colours help them to attract a mate. The males develop
a hump back and hooked jaws that are lined with small teeth.

The return of millions of salmon to the rivers where they were born is one of the world's most spectacular natural events. In some stretches of water there can be so many salmon that the water looks red.

44

Swimming up rivers takes huge effort. Rivers have small waterfalls and rapids that the salmon have to pass. Salmon may spend several days slowly making their way up small waterfalls, leaping distances of up to 1.7 metres at a time. They do this by leaping out of the water at speed, then beating their tail to get higher. This leaping and swimming against the flow of water is exhausting for them.

As well as natural obstacles, there may be weirs and dams that people have built across rivers. Fortunately, many dams have special passing places for salmon, called fish ladders, which allow the salmon to pass by.

There are other dangers too. The large numbers of salmon in the water attract predators such as grizzly bears. The bears love this time of year, when the salmon provide them with a feast of food. Large numbers of bears and their cubs gather in shallow water and along the river banks watching for salmon. They catch the fish with their large claws and quickly eat them. Eating a lot of salmon is essential for the bears' survival as they need to build up their fat stores to survive the cold winter.

weir

fish ladder

The circle of life

The salmon reach their spawning grounds in autumn. There, the females dig their nests and lay their eggs, which the males then fertilise. By now, the salmon are exhausted. They've not eaten for several weeks and have used their last reserves of energy to spawn. Sadly, most of these amazing fish die after the eggs are laid.

However, there are always a few females that survive this ordeal and they make their way back down the river to the sea, where they feed and recover. These females are called kelts. In a year or so, they will return to the river to spawn again.

The spawning areas are quickly littered with the dead bodies of the salmon. Their bodies attract other animals, especially grizzly and black bears, wolves, bald eagles, ospreys and otters. These animals **scavenge** on the remains. Other fish in the river join in the feeding frenzy too, pulling off chunks of flesh to eat.

This last stage In the life cycle of the salmon is critical to the well-being of the river. The dead salmon provide vital food for animals that have to survive through the long, harsh winters.

Not all the salmon are eaten. Some of their bodies rot and release nutrients into the water. These nutrients are used by the plankton at the bottom of the food chain. Trees and other plants that live along the banks of the river use the nutrients too, fuelling a new spurt of growth in spring.

Some of the dead salmon are carried away from the river by birds and bears and dropped in the surrounding forest. There, **decomposers** such as beetles, worms, fungi and bacteria break down the dead bits and the nutrients are released into the soil to be used by the forest plants.

By spring, all the dead bodies are gone and the alevins emerge
to start the cycle again.

Glossary

amphibians　animals such as frogs that lay their eggs in water but as adults live on land

currents　flows of water in definite directions through rivers, seas and oceans

decomposers　living things that help to break down dead and decaying matter, for example fungi and bacteria

diameter　a straight line that goes from one side of a circle to the other through its centre

dogfish　a type of shark

fertilised　when the male sperm joins with the female egg to produce a new animal

kidneys　organs in the body that take water and waste materials from the blood to produce urine

metamorphosis　a change in appearance in a life cycle, for example from tadpole to frog

nutrients　foods and vitamins that are needed for good health

predators　animals that hunt and eat other animals

pupa　the stage of an insect between larva and adult

scavenge　animals feeding on dead and decaying matter

spawning grounds　places where animals such as fish lay their eggs

tendrils　structures that coil around objects to hold on to them

Index

The life cycle of salmon

breeding pair

adult

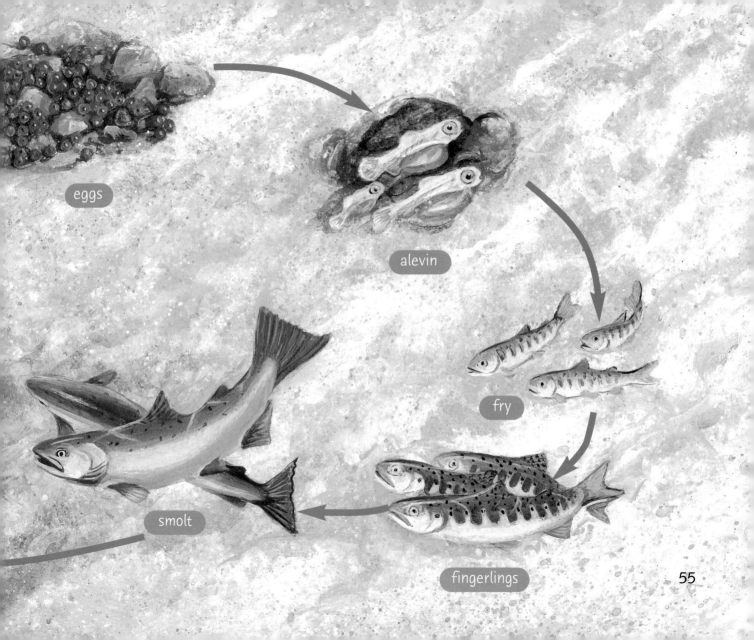

eggs

alevin

fry

smolt

fingerlings

55

Ideas for guided reading 🐾

Learning objectives: make notes on and use evidence from across a text to explain ideas; compare different types of information texts and identify how they are structured; use and explore different question types

Curriculum links: Science: Life cycles

Interest words: alevins, amphibians, currents, decomposers, diameter, dogfish, fertilised, fingerlings, food chains, kelts, kidneys, metamorphosis, nutrients, plankton, predators, pupa, scavenge, spawning, tendrils, smolts

Resources: whiteboard, ICT

Getting started

This book can be read over two or more guided reading sessions.

- Discuss what children think a life cycle is and write their ideas on the whiteboard. Use the image on the cover and the blurb to prompt them.

- Turn to the glossary and index and ensure children understand how to use them.

Reading and responding

- As a group, read to p5 and discuss which animals lay eggs and which give birth to live young. Can they come up with examples that aren't in the book?

- Ask children to continue to read independently to the end of the book, making notes on important information.

- Remind them that they can use diagrams and photographs from the book to support their notes, but they must use their own words to describe the information.

Returning to the book

- Using pp54–55 as a model, encourage children in pairs to tell each other the story of the life cycle of the salmon, referring to their notes for support.